THE GRAVEDIGGER'S ARCHAEOLOGY

Previous Letras Latinas / Red Hen
Poetry Publication Prize Winners:

2013: Dan Vera : *SPEAKING WIRI WIRI*

The Gravedigger's Archaeology

Poems

William Archila

Red Hen Press | *Pasadena, CA*

Book layout by Danielle Verde

Library of Congress Cataloging-in-Publication Data
Archila, William.
  [Poems. Selections]
  The gravedigger's archaeology : poems / William Archila.—First edition.
     pages ; cm
  ISBN 978-1-59709-371-2 (softcover)
  I. Title.
  PR9298.9.A73A6 2015
  811'.6—dc23
                        2014037126

The Los Angeles County Arts Commission, the National Endowment for the Arts, the Pasadena Arts & Culture Commission and the City of Pasadena Cultural Affairs Division, the Los Angeles Department of Cultural Affairs, the Dwight Stuart Youth Fund, the Ahmanson Foundation, and Sony Pictures Entertainment partially support Red Hen Press.

First Edition
Published by Red Hen Press
www.redhen.org

Acknowledgments

To the editors of the following journals and anthologies in which some of these poems or earlier versions, some under different titles, first appeared, I extend grateful acknowledgment.

American Poetry Review, "Three Minutes with Mingus"; *Borderlands: Texas Poetry Review*, "The Line"; *Burnside Review*, "Nicaragua in Black & White"; *Clackamas Literary Review*, "Self-Portrait with Train," "In the Pit"; *Cold Mountain Review*, "Caffeine"; *Copper Nickel*, "What I Leaned from a War Too Small to Notice," "Goya's Execution"; *The Cortland Review*, "Outhouse"; *Crab Orchard Review*, "Some Other Boy," "The Night John Lennon Died"; *Grist*, "Shells," "After Reading Hopkins"; *Kalina*, "Clandestine Territory"; *The Los Angeles Review*, "Of Soldiers & Cane Toads," "Dismantling the Sea"; *Luvina, University of Guadalajara Literary Magazine*, "Some Other Boy"; *Malpais*, "Alfa," "In the Pit"; *North American Review*, "After Mass"; *The Normal School*, "Lake Guija"; *Notre Dame Review*, "Self-Portrait as Hermes," "At the Gold Room with Orpheus," "The Gravedigger's Archaeology"; *Poet Lore*, "Small Thumb of a Poet"; *Portland Review*, "Atlacatl"; and *Southern Poetry Review*, "Dig."

"Self-Portrait with Train" has been anthologized in *New Poets of the American West*, Many Voices Press (2010), edited by Lowell Jaeger. "Caffeine" and "The Night John Lennon Died" will appear in the anthology *Two Countries*, edited by Tina Schumann. "Caffeine" was also selected by Writers at Work for their poem of the month.

For their comments and readings, thanks to Joe Millar, Joshua Robbins and Brian Simoneau. Many thanks to Carolyn Forché and B. H. Fairchild. Special thanks to Francisco Aragón, Letras Latinas and Red Hen Press. I also extend my sincere gratitude to Orlando Ricardo Menes for believing in these poems. My deepest gratitude goes to my beautiful wife Lory Bedikian for her love and moral support. This collection of poems would not be possible without her inspiring wisdom.

For my mother Margarita Alfaro
and my father Rolando Archila

Contents

To trust or not to trust a poet's voice is a crucial element in the relationship between reader and text, so I find myself appreciating, indeed respecting, the toughness with which William Archila renders the characters that populate his gritty poems: men, women, and children who struggle on the periphery of society, whether here in the US as immigrants (probably undocumented) or back home in Central America, in particular his native El Salvador, as part of the caste-like underclass. For example, we find the "copper children, dressed in rags, ashy knees" who "shine shoes, / military boots, bodyguards' shoes, / those who lap the slime off the street" ("In the Pit"). In the same poem there is a woman named Concha "selling gum & cigarettes, / bunching her lips like a coin purse."

Elsewhere we are shown in striking language another woman named Lety who runs a roadside stand: "fat jiggles under her arms, / her apron, smudged yellow ruffles & pineapples / for pockets, crumpled like a fallen flag" ("Grease"). While these descriptions are no doubt unflattering, even grotesque, they are precise, tonally restrained, their purpose not to shock us gratuitously but to elicit our sympathy because of the poet's fealty to the truth. The language has an undeniable beauty, subtly ironic, quirky too, as in the "smudged yellow ruffles & pineapples / for pockets." The image of the apron "crumpled like a fallen flag" is conceptually charged, triggering in the reader feelings of despair and hopelessness.

There is no denying that a certain bleakness pervades the collection, as when the poet asks in "Don Santiago" "who needs another elegy?" One might be inclined to read these words as tongue-in-cheek, a rhetorical question whose answer should be playfully affirmative, yet the poet's own response—"Even the gravedigger & his spade are dead"—effectively closes the poem with an assertion that evokes emptiness and futility. Nonetheless, the poet's mood is far more complex and nuanced, his vision much more Orphic than Sisyphean, such somber hardness counterbalanced by a ludic imagination that propels other poems toward transformation and redemption, such as in "Alpha" where Benny's garage is described as dysfunctional and disheveled (e.g., "a counter overstocked / with dull starters" and "dusty tailpipes piled like logs") but at the same time we encounter "the glow / of an altar" above the counter and the metaphor of the shop as "a dim cathedral smelling of gas." Benny's garage is thus transformed into a place of sacredness, of wonder, of awe, a chapel where the priestly mechanic can love "the crank of small gears, their bright silver teeth."

An immigrant who, as a young boy, fled the violence and chaos of El Salvador's civil war, Archila "crossed the border like a full / moon that rises over rooftops" ("The Line") and thereafter experienced the loss of his homeland as well as the traumas of assimilation. It is no wonder that questions of identity and belonging breathe an urgent passion into many of his poems, especially those that explore memory, which is paradoxically both a source of comfort and a source of pain; yet the poet perseveres in digging through the many strata of the past, as in the poem "Dig," a beautiful homage to Seamus Heaney's "Digging," where his father exhorts him to "Dig, son. Dig," a man who works by intuition, "without tape or yardstick, / without compass or pocket loop." A source of strength but perhaps of shame as well to the eleven-year-old Archila, this is the father "who had become a kitchen helper, pots & pans / burned black, the slow drag of chain smoke / as he waited for the bus, the cold breath / of the American pavement on his back" ("The Night John Lennon Died").

"Outhouse," another poem about remembrance that is powerfully poignant, recalls the murder of the poet's uncle: "It breaks her / to talk now, knowing her brother / was hacked to pieces, burnt down in an outhouse. I was five / when he leaned against the wall / plucking strings, each chord / like brown waters groaning / under the bridge, the moon / in the sky a spot of ash." It is a horrible event that no doubt needs to be remembered, but notice how this skillful, inventive poet transmutes memory into myth, crossing the border between the past and the imagined, specifically with the allusion to the tragic Orpheus, patron god of lyric poets. His mother's brother is the familial version of Victor Jara, a leftist Chilean singer tortured and murdered by the military junta in 1973 whose "guitar made of night, pluck[ed] / and strumm[ed] Latin / America, a continent tied in a knot, / black from ash" ("Small Thumb of a Poet"). Archila's attraction to myth, which richly complicates the theme of identity, whether personal or cultural, extends to other figures like Hermes, Hector, and even the Trojan Horse.

I likewise admire how this poet understands the fragility of memory, the tenuousness of the past, even when he admits the stubbornness of certain memories, as in the poem "Lake Guija," where he employs to brilliant effect the conceit of the puzzle in the process of recalling, more accurately reconstructing, a fleeting moment from his childhood: "It's a puzzle incomplete . . . bits & pieces / I glue together, then / break apart . . . the wreckage of the lake / unchained against my feet." I find insight and wisdom in these words. Archila's poetic voice is worthy of our trust.

The Gravedigger's Archaeology

They dug and heard nothing more;
they did not grow wise, invented no song,
thought up for themselves no language.
They dug.
—Paul Celan, "There Was Earth Inside Them"

THE GRAVEDIGGER

The Gravedigger's Archaeology

I am not one of Hamlet's gravediggers, not one of his clowns
but I've been making graves since I was ten, wielding the tools

to get back to the center of things, past stone and hardpan,
the one thousand minerals attached to body scraps.

I am not a mason, shipwright, or carpenter, but I know how
to house these remains, this skull that belonged to Chenca: his wet-dog face,

the way he'd spit on his hands, rub them together to slick back his hair,
how he always wanted to meet a schoolgirl in a blue & white uniform

but came home with his tail between his legs, always the same ache.
Sometimes I shovel rubble & gravel from a graveyard

behind a Mayan ruin, when I dig deeper, the earth turns black
so shiny it stains my fingers. Sometimes, I hit something solid,

rasping sounds tucked among a labyrinth of bones. A god
shrouded in root hairs & soil, copper sun twisted like a serpent

crowning the head, comes forth. All this, except for the right limb
contorted, foot sole touching the chest near the heart

as if it's understood, this ground is all it knows, same plot of ground
I excavate, loads carted away. This is no desecration

to lower a six-foot pine box where the relic made its resting place.
No cairn or cross to mark the spot. Everything I know is here.

That's why I've come down to claim my inheritance,
the torn & tormented arsenal, charred bits & pieces of ammo.

I've come to decipher the fragments, the broken gods of clay,
the maggots gorged on the lung's frame, to watch earth empty

its mouth, unfurl a forked tip, hair like, and the flesh to go limp
like a dishrag. They deserve a Christian burial, so they say.

When a man gets this low, waist-deep in dirt, he can hear
his countrymen plead for a fraction of land they could never have

unless they fled to the barracks, joined the movement underground,
at least that's the promise in the streets. Others simply pack

their bags and go beyond the bramble & barbed wire. Me,
there are days I cannot stand the noise, nor stand the filth

beneath my fingernails, nor shut out the wood creaking in my ears,
the scoops loaded loose onto the lid, making a muffled thud.

IN THE PIT

IN THE PIT

There's Concha selling gum & cigarettes,
bunching her lips like a coin purse,
always in flip-flops, heels nicked dry. If you talk to her
her voice carries the sound of hay chewed by cows.

See the man squatting on the gutter, coffee can
between his feet, he was a carpenter
until they broke him down with electricity,
psychology, then photographed, uncombed.

The muck of the river, where trash washes
into the gullet, tin huts choke on coils of smoke—
Here the morning aches like a cold chemical in the joints,
incision of gristle & fat, buries itself in the gut.

Those are buzzards holding meetings
over our heads, spiraling with wings spread wide.
They fill the stainless elevators with their smell,
conceive babies on sweat alone.

And the copper children, dressed in rags, ashy knees
staring at us, they shine shoes,
military boots, bodyguards' shoes, those who lap
the slime off the street. They cart packages,

they are underpriced, under ten, the children I mean.
This is where the street inhales, gasps for air,
raises its asphalt to the light
                              as if letting out
a circle of nothingness, a hole in the broken ground.

Of Soldiers & Cane Toads

I

They came back in their wrinkled uniforms,
stiff & numb, cut off from the broken echo
of the ocean, crash of salt & sand, pupils cracked

to the ash end of a coffin nail, a longneck
to pacify the bone-breaking cold of pins
& needles, a fever of slowly dying in corners

of bus stations, taking empty highways
to ghost towns, talking to no one.

II

They broke out over the murky water.
At first, just its head, gravel over the eyes,
then snout, black blotches down the rear.

Others followed, olive-gray, red-brown,
struggling between bent-back reeds,
the reeking rot of branches. We heard

the first croak among the foliage, metallic
like a small machine. Another one inflated
its lungs, puffing up, lifting its trunk off the mire.

We trekked the shallows, stuffing them
into jars, lids with three nail holes.

III

We never saw Will again. He collapsed,
the wall of his body locked up
in the old shack behind his parents' house

where he dropped into a couch
his brother says, a bottomless sleep
beyond the door. And Chepe, a guard

in a bank downtown, misses pointing the rifle
with the butt-end against his waist, the muzzle
always pointed forward. By nightfall, he's a barfly

and bouncer at the local tavern, telling
war stories if you buy him a double, hand curled
tight around his pistol as he speaks of the dead rotting

beneath the open books of the library, but today
he's a clown, breathing fire at the bus stop, gas pours
out of his mouth as he waits for the red light to flash.

IV

Goyo threw the jar from the top of a tree, crouched
over the toad and lifted its terrible weight, dumped it
in a ditch, a sewer pipe in its stagnant bottom.

The toad, wart skin spewing a milky fluid, dragged
itself out with two broken legs like a soldier crawling
over mudflats. I don't know how Goyo found his way

into the group, with his missing teeth, busted nose,
neck full of creases, just that we feared him
the way we feared soldiers, inching their way

through grasslands, gunstocks against shoulders.
When he joined the battalion, we unscrewed the lids,
let cane toads go, knowing they'd come back.

GREASE

Lety's roadside stand steams under two light bulbs
   like a wreck's burnt-out shell beside a fire.
   Her A.M. radio's broadcast bleeding news
   pours on for another hour. This morning's wrist
   slit again, as she rolls a ball of dough
   out of the bucket, flattens it between her palms
   as if clapping, adds water, more dough,
   wipes her forehead with the back of her hand,
the calloused bottoms of her feet throbbing.

Her life has gone like this for some time,
   this day's end plowing through half-eaten plates
   strewn on the table's weathered grain. She stuffs
   pork rinds & refried beans, sometimes bits
   of squash & cheese, closes the edges together
   to make a fist, kneads again. When she pounds
   the perfect circle, fat jiggles under her arms,
   her apron, smudged yellow ruffles & pineapples
for pockets, crumpled like a fallen flag.

This toasted smell, like a winter's wind that drags
   its tail through the fields, pulls a man named
   Licho out of the brushwood, his beard thick
   as stubble. He chews as if he has not eaten
   for days and now he can forgive his boss,

even give thanks for the chock-full of dimes
    still warm in his hands. She can see he's old
    by the way his eyes gleam, a farm machine
as if the years have withered through him.

He reminds her of an old machete now rusty,
    always dirty, always sweaty, whose blade has
    hacked down stalk many times in the open.
    She can tell he has slept under the dew, stretched out
    on a trash bag the size of his body, curled
    right up against a log, body heat as blanket.
    She can tell they were both burned, dark
    like charcoal, in the same oven. They both came
from the same sandals of tire & rope.

She browns him a few more, spoons pickled cabbage
    out of a jar, hands him a brown paper bag
    he carries into the oil of night. She watches
    him disappear, the way a road turns
    into a sloping hill, the branch's silhouette
    moving across his hat. She's thankful
    for the toasted smell seeped in his clothes,
    for the fuel in his belly, lard that oozes
out of his pores, grease protecting him from the cold.

CITIES

From the cabin, horse-face Hector,
   trucker from San Julian, shakes
his head in laughter, tells us to get back
   to work; we load Coca-Cola crates
from the truck bed, exhaust buildup
   clogged in our throats, the iron plate
of the midday sun pressing down
   on our backs, and Paco, with his knowledge
of cows & pigs, turns to me and says,
   "You'll remember this." We cart
 bottles of sugar water to shanties
   almost a mile from the highway shoulder,
our stop somewhere between Santa Ana
   & San Salvador. This is before 1980
and the coming of M-16s slung
   across soldiers' chests, before walls
crumbled into rubble, bodies tossed
   like garbage in the gutter. Winter
would bring rain like lead, ripping
   through branches, cups of flowers clawing
above the grassland, a sudden burst of blaze
   among gun barrels dripping with water.
Soon I would turn fifteen, hide in the thick
   of the foxtails with Evelyn, our skin
growing darker & darker like animals.
   In a year I would disappear, roll

across the interstate line, Los Angeles
　　to San Francisco, my truck packed
with cherries, plums & grapes crammed
　　in their boxes. When I see the men
with their wide-brimmed straw hats,
　　their bodies bent on the ranch, I think
of Paco collapsed behind the truck,
　　Evelyn beyond the scorched hills,
how the smoking factories burn all night,
　　how day falls into a thin film of smog
as I unload my cases, thread my way
　　through tunnels, where memory,
bottle caps crushed on the asphalt,
　　can't recall which street to steer by,
not even where to make my final stop,
　　how long before the highway ends.

THE LINE

I watch them climb the wall,
stumble over tarnished coils
under hills scorched in dry heat
shriveled up into stone. I remember
I jumped a barbed wire fence—
ropes of bristling spikes nailed
against the bark of a tree—
and found a small wooden cross
tilting on the roadway trench.
I know the body was not shipped
back to the family, given a funeral,
the news never reached the father
before he wandered the border towns
seeking his son, the mother
covering her face with an apron.
The small screen flickers on my face,
displays twenty men shackled, single-file
boarding a bus at daylight.
I often wonder about the father
too exhausted to sleep, scuffing
for miles, his journey erratic
as if he does not want to arrive,
the earth below his feet raspy
like ashes. The line stretches
on this page, forges a road
across countries, the entire

length of the coast, always
pulling me toward the hours
I crossed the border like a full
moon that rises over rooftops,
my back wet, the blades of the chopper
blasting wind & falling rain.

The Night John Lennon Died

I come down the thrashed mountain
repeating, "The Lord is my shepherd. I shall not want,"
my mother's hand over mine, the moon on guard,
wind slapping my face, smell of rain & trees
as we enter the states, fog rolling out
at daybreak, suburbs glazed in light—
a load of refugees coming out of the ravine
across streets, hiding behind parked cars
dripping with mist, bodies low & close,
creeping on the ground like soldiers over puddles.

My mother in her best clothes—Lee corduroy
jacket, Levi's jeans—carries a newspaper
close to her chest, the picture of a man
from Liverpool shot in front of his house.
I am eleven, running toward a father
who had become a kitchen helper, pots & pans
burned black, the slow drag of chain smoke
as he waited for the bus, the cold breath
of the American pavement on his back.

I never expected the next morning, grey & damp,
watching my father coming out of the wooden house.
I want to take the boy, who lost his dad in a gun blast,
say, "Here is mine, a man who left a country rift in half.
Here he is, defeated, this Salvadoran I will outgrow,

this one with the wet apron & yellow gloves."
I say nothing, not a single word, not even a sound
as he touches my head, my arms around his waist.

NICARAGUA IN BLACK & WHITE

It's 1980 in the photograph, a year
after the dictator's farewell. Peasants
tread behind the tightly stretched banner:

We are not birds that live in the air,
nor fish that live in the sea. We
are men who live from the land.

They wear baseball caps, straw hats.
Some of them raise their machetes
up in the air, others their fists.

The trees, lined along the way,
also seem to be spreading their branches,
arms flung open, leaves fluttering in light.

One boy on the roadside
mimics his father, his machete
held up like a flaming torch.

At ten, I could never find words,
my tongue knotted, phrases caught
in my vocal cords. I could not tell them

I wanted to lift my left fist, raise
dust on the shoulders of the roadside.
I could not confess that I imagined myself

beating my feathers around treetops,
that I wanted to flicker my tail
deep at the bottom of the lake,

dart through the dark waters,
that I only wanted to be a boy,
not the men buried in the land.

SOME OTHER BOY

I've stood at the bay, watched
the fishermen sail out at dawn, the roar

    of waves raging at the rocks, palm trees
    still dark. This is my first winter

in a city of ice, scrubbing walls,
pushing a long mop down halls, scuffed floors,

    wandering the buildings after hours
    emptying trash cans till the bodies come

with no sound, flat on the frost
like bones of dead trees piled in the dark.

    I was only a boy, still shy
    still alone, when I peered my eyes

over the small window of the coffin, stared for a minute:
the face of chalk, nailheads of the eyes—death

    a rock, solid & strong,
    always there in the cup of my hands.

I see how it lives, how it swells with sand,
roots from the bottom of the sea, how it washes out

pieces of wood, fish heads,
the vein of a leaf sunk into the strand.

I think of the dead, how they will never feel
the curve of the bay, how it foams

at the mouth, throbs at a country
I fled years ago. It doesn't matter.

It's all gone. Today, some other boy comes
to the sea, says its name better than I did.

CLANDESTINE TERRITORY

It could mean retreating
to the heavy trace of spent
cartridges, smoke from hilltops
scudding through houses.

It could mean going back to bodies
dumped in a black lava bed,
the moon smoking like a tire
while they lie torn & swollen.

It's an art of departure really,
very much like the exile who flees
town without a word, catches
a few hours of shut-eye in the woods.

Think of the working immigrants
while they pass the salt
over steaming bowls of soup
or while they wait in line to cash

their checks. They restrain its name
and keep their five-foot distance.
Come holidays, they travel
across freeways, visit relatives.

Stories trickle out with gin from a bottle,
fathers & mothers in the forties,
when films were black & white
they say, when you could scroll

the A.M. dial for a drama, get a load
of the lovers kiss, a crackle
or the long curl of the surf, their static
shattering like waves on the coast.

Then it's on the pickup truck again,
back to the crew & framing hammer,
raise another wall, swing a pick
all day till they're waist-deep in the trench.

It's a matter of finding ways
around it, not to digress nor head
directly toward the subject, break
the conversation short, the way

winter pulls the sun away so early
in order to avoid its name, the way
civilians slow down their pace
to elude guards standing on watch.

Say its name and their memories turn
to hiding on rooftops like a sharpshooter.
Say rock or say dirt and the weeds
& thistles rise like bleached bones.

Say it and it conjures a country
unknown or simply impossible,
a funnel of smog, a land of ashes
they could call clandestine territory.

CAFFEINE

Sometimes it's a full orange hanging in the skyline
a road full of guitars and cigars

or a raindrop sliding down my mother's eyebrow.
My father, on the fire escape, reads

the black grounds collapsed in his cup.
"It's one in the morning somewhere in Central America,"

he says, "I sit in the hospital bed next to your mother,
San Juan De Dios, September 9, 1968.

You're wrapped in my arms
as she dips her finger in coffee, rubs it on your lip.

Drop by drop, a map spreads in your belly."
This could be true, and I want to believe it,

the whole weight of a nation that gathers
in the distant blue tropics, its whole weight in a cup.

The two of us watch the smog fill this sprawl of LA,
headlights & taillights pouring into the freeway.

It's the same story that drags me to work,
my head bobbing as the bus hisses, exhales exhaust,

song that unloosens me when I come home
tired, fall like coins on the dusty floor,

away from sinks filled with dishes & pans,
when I am with him drinking that mud, I dissolve

into the place of my birth, a slip of land by the shore.

VIGIL

Mama Juana leaves a glass
of cold water on the window sill

to quench the exhausted tangle
of roots he carries, black broken
branches he drags across the blind alleys.

He was the green-eyed man who smoked
at the corner, the one with no stop sign
or lamp post, cigarette dangling from his lips.

You could spot the orange glow
floating in the twilight, you could hear
his guitar crooning of ox carts, of creaking wheels.

The evening he disappeared a cluster
of monarchs came to die at the door,

a thousand wings crumpled & crushed,
buried in flowerpots. We sat in church

sifting through photo albums, battered faces
in black & white, each with a thread of words
unrolling the tattered names, folded
hills where the bodies remain.

Dusk like a raven's wing falls
over the house. I'm here, Uncle,
sneaking barefoot in the dark, behind

the barred window, you know the one.
I'm the boy holding a glass of cold water

looking down the sidewalk for a sign,
smoke fluttering from a flicker of light.

After Mass

I see him calling for water to soothe
the blood & gristle that's dried,
but no one comes, not even the priest
in his robe like a frightened ghost.
   He rests in a glass case, bleak & bare,
skin pale blue, almost gone to mold,
the nail holes of his feet disintegrating.
His features, cropped by a wig's curls, unlike
any hair I've seen before, drown in silence.

My aunt tells me I will grow fangs, horns
if I don't visit the basilica, my claws, hooks
clinging to the roof—I will howl like a wolf
in the rain if I don't plead at his feet.
   But no one comes to my bed, when I'm thinking
he's alive in that coffin, chewing the insides
of my mind, that gray matter clicking,
but never understanding this plastered
Christ hammered above my head.

Atlacatl

At the crossroads, the statue
of a warrior leans forward, gaze
of an eagle reading the horizon,
headdress a plumage of feathers.

In the vein between the eyebrows,
the pellet pierced the jaguar pelt of his body.

You can hear the iron men
with spur & muzzle, hooves
clopping harder as they gallop
against gravel, heat rising
like the snort of an underground animal,
wide nostrils steaming.

They say he stood on a headland,
blew on a seashell, disc
of the sun raging above, a sound
that thickened the air,
bruised it to darkness, turned
the entire contour of Cuzcatlán
into a smoking volcano.

What drove women to descend
into rivers, their long strands
of black hair along the bank,

what caused leaves to sink
to the bottom, central ridge break
into threads, minerals fossilized
on slabs of rock, then fractured,
what parched the rows of corn,
amputate the trunk of the moon,
shattered, blasted to a stump,
falling like a forest in fire.

Now they leave only a statue.
On the national coins, their faded profiles
& tarnished helmets, their forked beards
the color of grime.

Near Downtown

They want to be anywhere else
but here, slouched on their chairs
as the sun midway across the sky
opens its mouth, round & empty.
The mister runs through
another scripted lesson, his voice
a monotonous bell clanging
in their ears. He also wants
to be somewhere else, Paris
or Spain, but instead he's stuck
inside a meat-locker for a room,
a building with no bell tower
or archway, but hot dog trays,
milk cartons littering the hallway.
The clock ticks away. Juventino
staggers in, dragging the cuffs
of his pants, his lumberjack
jacket buttoned at the top, revealing
the white triangle of his shirt,
belt buckled at the waist. He's here
once a week, the others spent
with his dogs blazing blunts
across the yard, shouts & growls
rolling to the curve. On dictionaries
he tags his name, knowing
when he walks out, past

the flag wind-whipped on the pole,
he won't return. Enough hours
staring at a blank page. He'll take
the potholed alleys behind
the overpass, tenements that soar
like smoke stacks, past the patrol
to the metro station, where he'll join
the swaying crowds down the tunnel,
his white shirt like a small ghost
descending into the underground.

Alfa

I step through the cave, trail of exhaust.
What seem to be lurid organs fastened
to the wall like hooked meat
in a butcher shop burnt camshafts, manifolds.
"All they need is a good cleaning," he says,
as he slides under the tank.

In Benny's garage, the glow
of an altar burns above a counter overstocked
with dull starters, cylinder heads laid flat
cold as ashes, dusty tailpipes piled like logs.

Ever since he laid eyes on a GTV, 1968,
he always wanted to work on cars
even though in Metapán
mechanics were considered drunks,
drunk as a fart, he tells me. He loved
the crank of small gears, their bright silver teeth.
It was like a religion with him,
the shop a dim cathedral smelling of gas.
As long as he could buy a plateful of black beans,
the bus fare back home, he didn't care.

I listen to the Romeo owners
in the oil-stained lot of ripped tires, the black
chassis of a burnt-out roadster. They swap tales:
where to scavenge for a cracked dashboard,
how far to drive for a fender,
no matter how deeply rusted.

After an hour & a half, his forehead gleaming
with sweat, shirt smeared with grease,
he's pulled out the spark plugs,
replaced three gaskets,
two frayed belts & a coil wire—
I watch the golden cross chained
around his neck, hanging over the motor.
It glints, flickers like a timing light.
"All we need," he says, "is the spit of God."

Dismantling the Sea

The rains have continued
for five days now

and there's no end in sight,
not with the sky slit open,

the torrential downpour
leaving black branches, muddy walls

& dead dogs along the riverbank.
Of course, I should have known

anything's possible anytime.
I was told about it in church

& school, but I never paid
any respect, not with switchblades

roaming the markets,
not with lead & fire

wanting the taste of hair
& flesh, factories spreading

their industrial filth
into the waters—a bloated cow, legs up.

Of course, I didn't know
the war machine reappears

at least every decade
to splinter the backbone & chassis

of a people so small, so poor
so barely audible

even to its neighbors
who arrive simply to inspect,

delegate the same old want
of dominion, the want of land.

It never ceases to amaze me
the way history babbles

into the night, a darkness
that doesn't give a damn

like this rain, five days straight, then not
a drop, except the sea overflowing.

What I Learned from a War Too Small to Notice

To lie awake all night under the bed, stare
      at the springs, study of coils & hooks,
ironwork's constellation disarmed
      into a shattered landscape, light bulbs
doused with the grumbling sound of artillery.

      To cut off my breath, for at least a minute,
choke the dumb thump of the heart's vein,
      then release, count the beat's thud, a muffled
blow like driving a nail into soft wood,
      one hit, one blue nail splitting the heart.

Night sounds magnified. Every foot's scratch,
      every backdoor squeak or cracked tile
on the rooftop was a loose private, down
      from the shanties they came, dressed
as civilians, triggers burning like live coals.

      My childhood of 1980
learned to take cover during shootouts,
      mold itself into the cut-corner
of the curb, lie half drowned in the street's gutter,
      resembling a half-rotting animal.

My childhood of 1980
　　　saw my mother hanging wash
on a cold morning, her house dress wet
　　　from the load of clothes, my eyes on the church's
belfry, a needle in the sun's match flare,

　　　my eyes on pews overturned, saints fractured
on the floor, on their boots, black as a furnace,
　　　beside the altar the blunt weight
of the gun, the blade embracing the back,
　　　their faces covered with brown paper bags.

I didn't know what it meant. I didn't know
　　　I could never leave this war. Even now,
I am the buckets of water splashing
　　　on cobblestones, the dapples of mud,
that clothesline trembling in the wind.

Self-Portrait with Train

It was like metal collapsing
at my feet, the clank & roar

announcing one hundred tons of iron
plying down the track. No doubt

it was more like a drunken wreck
up front in the engine, bailing

at full throttle when everything's red,
coals with a core of glowing fire,

not the sort that burns in a flame
but a deep heat like ore in a furnace.

There's nothing like it,
no satisfaction so complete

in its velocity, such monotonous force
pulling through the land. I've been here before

where a man remembers
the plug run he rode as a boy,

windows down, wind swollen
with rain—a shot of smoke

overwhelming the sky—
and it's almost impossible to forget

when the rails' red lights block
early morning's stop-and-go,

wheels popping and grinding,
wood & steel lining up the roadway

but now, no sound comes
from the engine driving on

beyond the green bay, no sounds
from me, except these stacked logs

chained to their flat beds, pushing
with no meter or rhyme, no form

for the line of cars carrying their cargo.
Let me begin again

with the brush & weed trails
I came upon in Coatepeque,

stray dogs rambling along the ditch,
country girls & their clay pitchers

perched on their heads—they live
in the coffee fields, the earth's cracks.

This time when the coal burner stalls
at the fork and the boxcars come

to a dead stop, a pair of oxen plodding
through the mud, pulling the plow,

I know I'll be home
knowing that nothing changes

at the first break of light,
that when the doors slam

someone will step into the bed of gravel
and the shirtless boy standing

in the doorway will get smaller,
smaller as the train pulls away.

THE NIGHT WATCHMAN

At the Gold Room with Orpheus

Bent over a shot of whiskey, hat cocked,
cigarette cut between his teeth, he's always there

around eleven, after guarding a parking lot three levels down
beneath the low columns of the oracle. They say

his Eurydice was claimed by the netherworld,
dragged into the cavern's chasm, across choppy waters,

boat dandled among the fiery fingers of a furious river,
burnt gas & soot everywhere. The winter of 1989,

he knows too well, thick trail of charge in the air,
his wife scattered like seeds among the rustle of ants,

sandals tossed among volcanic rocks, houses flattened,
broken & forgotten, a spent fire for three-headed dogs.

He leans over the rail, mutters something
the bartender has refused to understand,

something about Hades and the Lord of the Dead.
Some say he was exiled from his people, left

empty handed without his young bride, a face
he can no longer see in the spiral of a hubcap

when he hunches on a stool, validates stubs,
watching the stream of rolling cars. Eyes half shut,

he bobs alone by the light of a jukebox,
shuffling, shuffling, the smell of booze clinging

to his suit, his left palm flat on the stomach, right arm
half raised, holding Eurydice's imaginary hand.

OUTHOUSE

It's him again, a man clean
as a knife, plodding among fields
sprouting to the sky, pack
of smokes nestled in the folded
sleeve of his arm, a firm grip
on his guitar. I want to say
his sister waits for him
in a dress of yellow poppies.
He doesn't recognize me,
his sister's boy wandering
the black hills of Candelaria
searching for his green eyes.
He doesn't know she ran
across city-mountains, following
the steps of a brother, how
her house crumbled flat,
trees hacked down, nothing left,
not even dry land beneath
her feet. I can't remember
how long I stood as smoke
covered the street corner
and mother stubbed out
his cigarettes. It breaks her
to talk now, knowing her brother
was hacked to pieces, burnt down
in an outhouse. I was five

when he leaned against the wall
plucking strings, each chord
like brown waters groaning
under the bridge, the moon
in the sky a spot of ash.

Small Thumb of a Poet

I find her in the bedroom, tired & pale,
homesick for her old republic,
cocking one ear to Victor Jara,
her transistor radio, compact
speaker broadcasting a sound
    like burning paper,

his guitar made of night, plucking
and strumming Latin
America, a continent tied in a knot,
black from ash.
    I learned to love
this music as a boy, the same folk songs
at work on the turntable,
wearing out from repeated playings,
too many times, losing meaning.

She drank coffee with bards,
her lines short,
well carved, hammered and cut—

my mother, who wanted to be
the small thumb of a poet,
the belly of her people, shrunk,

rising and falling
like that of a dog.
          But tonight
she tells me she longs for the spot
where the summer grass bends
and the green swell rolls above the surf.

I tune in. Her voice forges
round rows of corn, sunlight crushing
into meadows. I pay close attention to weeds
shooting long, spiraling up like wheels,

the gang of peasants, street workers
armed with picks and trowels coming down
the mount, the light of El Salvador
hoisted over the house she built.

CUMBIA

That spiral of brass I left behind
in a wooden crate, rolling sounds of marimba
& accordion, tobacco & rum, drums that come
     from the swelling rhythms of the sea.

There's the song about the wet rooster
in the kitchen or Angulo & his rattlesnake,
bass line right up front till daybreak,
     the Colombian ones, of course, a tone

like a horse ride through the mountains,
though the best one I heard was on the way
to Chalate, up from the coast, the bus rattling
     down the cut of a two-lane highway,

cane fields trailing both shoulders. Passengers
half asleep lean on one another like sacks of corn.
When the radio blasts a cumbia thick as lard,
     women in their tight dresses step & pivot,

swing their curves into men, moon faced,
glasses full of rum & Coke in their grips.
They crash into each other, like waves
     thrashing against the gulf. A chorus

of laughter bounces off the roof as hail starts
to clatter on the tin top. Some stumble, some holler
when the driver honks along the bend. The bus
    lit like a ballroom slides into the ocean.

LABOR

He's been pounding the rutted face
of the mountain for hours, the curve
of his shirt gashed with sweat,

the sledge tearing down the boulder, grunt
by grunt, till the flakes pierce his lungs,

just like his fathers gutted the earth,
just like they knocked out sparks from the rock,
built tunnels, cities they could not inhabit,

nothing but bold steel
& rockfire, nothing but the rousing,
roof-shaking house of blues

he plays at sundown
on his doorstep, guitar nestled in the belly,
bare feet tapping against the porch

as he plucks the wires, hollers
about the Southern Pacific
railroad pulling across the tracks,

the boss in shades giving
orders from a long black car,
back-breaking mills, factories & docks,

but he's only a foot, a pair of arms
hard & knotted, legs apart
as the pick arcs around the shoulders, breaks

into rock, always the lowdown phrase
always delivering the punch, the clever turn,
the sun's gonna shine in my back door one day.

Dog Days

for Lory

At forty I live in a two-room
bungalow with no AC. My wife & I
sleep with the fan buzzing all night,
a spray bottle by the bedside.

I have a recurring dream of a cat
napping in a four-room English Tudor
with a full line cooling system,
the owner away in an office job.

I always wake up groggy & cranky
to work in a brick building, teaching kids
grammar, the windows wide open,
the heat wave rolling against our faces.

We turn off the lights and sit in the gloom
despite what the principal says. We flip
through pages of the north, Jack London
up in the snow caps, and keep drinking

from our warm, plastic bottles.
In the lounge, the adults keep gulping
iced coffee. The day is long & muggy,
each thought a drop of sweat

sculpted & chiseled. When I come home
my wife & I kiss, too hot to embrace.
I can smell the frustrating hours
of job-hunting in her long, black hair.

We shower, read *A Room with a View*
to remember our courting days of winter,
the fan turning, blowing hot air.
Sometimes I catch a gleam in her cheek,

and I want to hold it like a firefly
in a jar. When I say it to her
the lid is the night and the firefly,
its clumsy flight, us lost in a barley field.

When I open the jar, the lid moves
like a door hinge to our Tudor house.
We're in an English Garden, books open
on our laps, the rain about to fall.

Self-Portrait as Hermes

I'm not sure what I like about it, a red barn
       shooting up beyond the pasture's fence, where rain gathers,

the semi's tires grating down the blacktop.
       I can lose myself in the oak's bark, trunk overrun with moss

and then the cow, belly plumped with black patches, probing its muzzle
       into the mud-rooted flowers. I can stand here for hours,

stranded by the shoulder, my wheels exhausted from gridlock,
       its littered boulevards, which once, in their golden days,

held a promise, almost heaven flung, now a series of oil-streaked chuckholes.
       I want to cross, but the barbed wire holds me back, sends me back

to the boiling hood, wondering how long before the cruiser notices
       the radiator's siren. The crows know this,

the visitor trespassing, and they're right. So many have left
       their urban sprawl to stare at what once was a probability,

no longer theirs. This morning's frost melting
       on the asphalt is not mine. The stack of rotted wood sound asleep,

an ache for the dying day. I can feel the weariness, the industry's
    vertebrae-cracking frenzy. I must head back to cog wheels,

wire and grime, forget what beltways
    and canals have never known, what I used to know,

once when I had wings on my feet, when I ran down winding ways,
    cutting through thickets, hairs curling along my spine,

lost among the flocks of sheep, more like a god than a man.

After Reading Hopkins

Unable to sleep, I wander the house
casting out lines in the dark
as if standing on a shipwreck
or a church that's been bombed.
   The cluster of words falls like rocks
at my feet, where I stumble
toward a room that's always locked,
a block of letters chopped into the hardwood.

I go through the dictionary, massive knot
of thoughts, but nothing comes undone.
I'm a solitary figure in so much white
   space, making a little sound,
a pagan song, tapping the beat on the wall,
the floorboards creak as I open the door.

Goya's Execution

He must've died in the backwoods
  with the ants, the stinking flies,
   the owl's wing where dusk came in the shape
of hands, the color of clods clumped

between the knuckles. He must've died
  on the roof, the sky dark like a Colossus,
   a sheep's head impaled on a tree, eternally
cluttering his mind, distorted, incarcerated.

Maybe he faced the firing squad's stiff line,
  steel column of shako headgear, bayonets & barrels
   at point-blank range. A lantern threw
a slice of light, yellow ocher tinged on the wreckage.

No, he knelt among the matted sap,
  entirely lit, eyes locked in a hunted look
   like a creature chased down an open field
cornered at the foot of a cliff, growling.

He must've died a hundred times
  when every creeping thing that crept
   upon the earth formed spittle at the chops,
every bastard starving in a barren field

cursed the gaudy gold & red of the crown, a landscape
    complete save for the burst of lead plugged
    in the ribcage. No ocean gray can wash off
the weight of the stench lying low in the thicket,

the night's bone hovering over the steeple
    when he flung his arms wide before the click
    of the cap, the black splattered by a flash of light,
forked hands reaching for the cold pan of a star.

Still Life with Fish

I slit the belly with a jackknife,
    pull out the guts, throw it
        into the bucket. I can taste

grease, knobs of garlic,
    tomato, onion chopped, fish head
        & spine on my tin plate,

half a lemon like the sun.
    The smell of frying fish
        enters my nostrils, carries

me back to the shore. You'd think
    they'd stop, but they keep
        hitting my bait. It's gruesome

the way they thrash, gush
    among the waters, sliver of blood
        caught in the eye. Fish

always remember the swell
    the way oars creaking
        in rowlocks remember the trees.

They remember the floating kelp
      that tangle at the surface
            the way the hull recalls

the buck of the wave.
      I sometimes think
            of letting the plated fins flare

again, drown below the current,
      cold-blooded animal hooked
            by the crook of its jaw, fat piece

of lead sucking the air
      so heavy & red. Nothing
            but gills & scales,

dorsal wings feather-like.
      It slips out of hand, streamlined,
            tail flapping on deck.

STRAY

I don't know how I found him
the other day, but there he was
dumped in a ditch, stiff & bloated,

his pathetic fur charred in clumps,
face black like a bucket of tar,
his wide-open jaw cracked.

I thought of my childhood,
how once I saw a man with his bare nails
scoop a patch in the fields,

out of the realm of roots
unearth the toys, the rib cage
still clinging to its shirt.

The rope pulling tighter
at the knot in his stomach
always led him to burial grounds

overgrown with flat grass, flowers lank
turning to rust. Sometimes he pissed
on stones, scratched the moss

or fell asleep among the elms,
a halo of flies leaping
around the snout, legs quivering

as if tearing up the lawn,
digging his claws in the turf
until he hit the trace of a bone.

I felt as if a part of me
that had been asleep for years
began to throb, a swelling sound

bellowing out of my throat.
Nothing came out, not a sound
and he never cocked an ear

when I first spotted him
behind the brush, coming out
of the woods, reeking of dawn.

Study with Horse

When I measure spoonfuls of coffee,
two sugars, boil the water, my mornings
float on empty pockets of space,
a solitary raft anchored at my deck.
No passengers. No captain, except
a pale, blue horse, shoeless, clops down
the gangplank. Its muzzle dried
with brash, nostrils covered in cinder,
crest color of fog, flank scarred
with crust thick as bark. On the boards,
the roll & drop of the belly. I throw
buckets of water, scare off the flies,
its eyes glint like the sea.

＊

All the rubble collapses on me,
splintered wood, twisted metal beams,
the weight of the debris utterly exhausted.
Over the houses, I hear the drone
and I want to go out among the pines,
wandering on all fours like a creature
sniffing the far fields, hooves breaking
down needles, imagining the snow
melting into a clearing, the tarpaper sky
scraped with rips of light.

＊

Some still don't know the perimeter
between spent shells & a fistful of seeds
between a pile of rubble & a tangle of roots
and it will take an afterlife for some to believe.
Tell them the horse is dead. Tell them
I'm staying inside this animal's cold clay
because I demand the earth's daily bread,
because I demand a downpour
for the burning roof, and then nothing
but dawn, a tint of pale blue,
swept away by the shape of leaves,
all winter long the smoldering harness.

GEOGRAPHY LESSON

The frame I sketch on the open page
   resembles the flight of a sparrow
maybe foliage lurched against a tree
   or just a puddle in the alleyway.

I form one great lake, completely landlocked
   or is it two lakes? The peaks, if there are any,
bare their rigid veins in the white light.
   I've read its size appears

slightly larger than the state of Maryland
   or is it the state of Massachusetts?
Does it matter? It's smaller than an anthill.
   The topography, that's another story.

My pencil dots the watercourse, coffee
   beans placed in crooked lines,
branching out like the human nervous system.
   I trace its boundaries, coordinates,

short reaches across an isthmus
   and see a small wooden house on fire.
So many flames, so many tiny soldiers,
   smudges of red. I write ten letters

along the grid and the narrow country
        crams itself to the side of the coast.
I hear it in the rotor wash, in the rounds
        & ash crunched between my teeth.

Even home begins on a piece of paper,
        when the sharp tip of a pencil drives
its blade into the surface, digs out
        the relics—the drab flecks of crust.

SHELLS

They loaded their guns and shot
in the air—in the heat of light,
without praying to a god
of gold, wood or stone.

Pellets wailed. Dull cases
sprawled on the floor.
They lined them up on the dirt.

They shot a boy, a dog.
All the seeds in their heads
raised their flags.

They shot
without knowing trees from men,
without feeling the heat
in the palms of their hands.

In their sleep
they think they hear a shot.
In their sleep, the brush
& scrub grow over them,
tall yellow grass falls on them.

A hand plants a lead—deep,
genuine, complete seed of brass.

The muck bares its teeth,
mold smells & slugs,
a soiled tongue pulls
from a dank throat
—the rough face of clay.

They dug their graves.
The first day of heavy rain,
they shot, carried their rifles
like brooms and shot.

Line them up on the dirt.

DON SANTIAGO

Death always came to neighbors
just before dawn broke open, the sky
a steel grayness against the street,

the candle's dripping vein
glowing for the great dead,

always more with the coming days,
always more powerful than birds,

white as lime, white as chalk
sloshing through puddles.

The family does not live anymore.
They exist. They seemed lonely
as the barks of a dog.

What if I say this isn't an elegy,
but a recollection of Don Santiago,

a grave-maker & his sod-cutter,
and if I continue, the funeral band

will strike a note? There'll be an encore,
a priest & sermon for the spring.

Forget the pine box. Forget the altar
& the screaming like hogs
stuck in the bellies. I'll curse

dawn turning pale over the houses,
the streets strong & monotonous,

the discharge of lead like white slate
eating me alive from the stomach.

It's true, who needs another elegy?
Even the gravedigger & his spade are dead.

The Night Watchman

The afternoon they buried the sergeant

I saw buzzards hunched on the branch
of a twisted tree, their wings blotting out
the sun, carrying a heavy heat, as if

an animal had died in the alley,
something with cotton balls corked in the mouth.

The train rattles its skeleton.

They come from a heat-pulverized town,
women & their faces gnarled like oak trees,
children burrowed asleep on their shoulders.

The drunk, foul breath, flounders along the path,
brown paper bag clutched in his grip,

prostitutes from cheap hotels, and the priest
sings his mass, his face shivering
the way cow skin shivers under flies.

The great bell of Christ has rung.

No birds sing in full-throat, just two fistfuls
of crushed flowers & clay, lots of clay.

They found the body in an abandoned
factory, beheaded, cut in pieces,
left in plastic garbage bags.

One more time, the pallbearers hook the rails.

Midnight, darker than compost,
cracks in two, and through the opening,
rain eats dirt, keeping me inside with candles.

In January, the earth hardens
like iron, no hole can be dug,

rats crawl the dank, dark pipelines,

but with this heat pressing down,
flattening the weeds, this humidity that opens
every pore, you can smell the thickness

of buzzards sleeping, climbing in circles,
another sergeant in a garbage bag.

The dark scavengers pick on a toe.

Lake Guija

The ground & sky blow fire,
a clue the devil's quarters
must be up ahead.

Aunties whose voices are frayed
from cigarettes & coffee
chatter the tempo
of a language long forgotten.

I refuse to forget these women
Soon, they'll be gone in skiffs
casting their nets among the waves
washing out to the shore.

In the late-night blackout
their words will rise
as if deep from the bottom
of a well.
          Mid-July.
No one around, but a rooster
pecking pebbles on the rough grass.

It's a stubborn memory, I know,
a town split by railroad tracks
where the great green waters groan.

Sometimes, I want to follow
their path, step off the tar
and chase the barren trail
that carves the mountainside,
but I no longer fit those shoes.

It's a puzzle incomplete,
a wooden slat missing in a bridge
that clatters beneath the wheels
of a passing pickup.

These are bits & pieces
I glue together, then
break apart, when the town darkens
and I'm standing in the sand,
the wreckage of the lake
unchained against my feet.

Three Minutes with Mingus

When I read of poets & their lives,
    son of a milkman & seamstress, raised
in a whistle-stop town or village, a child
    who spent his after-school hours deep
in the pages of a library book, I want to go
    back to my childhood, back to the war,
rescue that boy under the bed, listening
    to what bullets can do to a man, take him
out of the homeland, enroll him in school,
    his class—size ten—unfold the fables
of the sea, a Spanish galleon slamming up
    & down the high waters. This is why
I write poems, why I prefer solitude
    when I listen to your lazy sound
of brass on the phonograph. You give
    language to black roosters & fossil bones,
break down phrases between the LA River
    & the yellow taxi cabs of New York.
I picture you in Watts, the 240-pound
    wrath of a bass player building up steam,
woodshedding for the strictly segregated
    hood, those who seek a tiny shot of God,
digging through hard pan, the hammer's
    grunt & blow. I need a gutbucket of gospel,
the flat land of cotton to catch all those

Chinese acrobats bubbling inside your head.
When I think of the day I will no longer
    hold a pencil within my hand or glance
upon the spines of my books, I hear
    Picasso's Guernica in your half-choked
cries, a gray workhorse lost in a fire's
    spiraling notes, a shrieking tenor sax
for the woman falling out of a burning house.
    I want to tell you if I wrote like you pick
& pat in *Blues & Roots*, I would understand
    the caravel of my childhood, loose,
without oars or sails, rolling on the swells
    of a distant sea. That's all I got, Mr. Mingus.
I give you the archaeology of my words,
    every painstaking sound I utter when I come
to the end of a line, especially the stressed
    beats of a tiny country I lost long ago.

DIG

DIG

I can tell you this much because I
    always begin with picks & shovels,
pencils & spoons, because I always
    return as a worm, six feet below,
    breeding a thing of leather & bone,
because the skin breaks over the nose,
belly sinks into a ditch of gas.

I can tell you what rose to the surface
    because of the arrowheads washed
& catalogued, because of the mountains
    crumpled like butcher paper, graver
    & vessel found in the strata, because
of the ravines broken off into chasms,
releasing fossils back into the sea.

And if there's more, it'll be my father,
    always trudging uphill, lugging
his two hundred pounds of flab,
    exhausted, nostalgic & melancholic,
    because come daybreak, he'll be at it again,
his shirt hanging on a branch, spade turning
the earth, exposing the loam to light.

And if there's truth in work, I learned it
    from him, among the junkyards

of auto parts, brake drums & pistons burned,
  in the preserves he delivered as a boy,
  exiled from childhood, from Munich
to Morazán, from the curl of a flugelhorn
to the spirals in a sundial or weathervane.

If there's more to say, it's because I loved
  in fathoms & groundwork, in hieroglyphics
that slip through a hole in the wire fence
  in trochees & dactyls, the volume
  of the ocean, the eye of a whale sounding,
daguerreotype of a leviathan
thrashing, the captain to the wheel strapped.

I can tell you this much because it's always
  my father who handles the claw hammer,
screwdriver speckled with rust, because
  it's my father, without tape or yardstick,
  without compass or pocket loop,
who tells me, lying under the house,
cutting a trench for the pipe, *Dig, son. Dig.*

Biographical Note

William Archila is the author of *The Art of Exile* (Bilingual Review Press, 2009), which won an International Latino Book Award in 2010 and was honored with an Emerging Writer Fellowship Award by The Writer's Center in Bethesda, MD. He has also been awarded the Alan Collins Scholarship at the Bread Loaf Writers' Conference. His poems have appeared in *AGNI, American Poetry Review, Notre Dame Review, The Georgia Review*, among others, and have been featured in *Poetry Daily*. His book was featured in "First Things First: The Fifth Annual Debut Poets Roundup" in *Poets & Writers*.

Printed in the USA
CPSIA information can be obtained
at www.ICGtesting.com
JSHW081637101123
51868JS00005B/285

9 781597 093712